Contemporary Design in Metalwork

Also by S H Glenister

CONTEMPORARY DESIGN IN WOODWORK
Volumes One and Two

Contemporary Design in Metalwork

Brian Larkman
with **S H Glenister** F Coll H

John Murray Fifty Albemarle Street London W 1

Printed in Great Britain by The Camelot Press Ltd., London and Southampton, and published by John Murray (Publishers) Ltd.

Contents

Acknowledgements

A book of this kind would be impossible without the willing co-operation of a great number of people. The authors are indebted, therefore, to all those craftsmen, designers, manufacturers and educational bodies who have responded so readily to their many requests. Thanks are especially due to the following:

The Council of Industrial Design
The Society of Industrial Artists
The Craft Centre of Great Britain
The Worshipful Company of Goldsmiths

also

Österreichisches Institut für Formgebung, Austria
National Industrial Design Council, Canada
Dansk Kunstaandvaerk, Denmark
Finnish Design Centre, Finland
Rat für Formgebung, Germany
Instituut voor Industriele Vormgeving, The Netherlands
Associazione per il Disegno Industriale, Italy
Norsk Brukunst, Norway
Svenska Slojdforeningen, Sweden
Schweizerischer Werkbund, Switzerland
American Society of Industrial Designers, U.S.A.

Failure to include a particular photograph should not be taken to imply disapproval of the design; the reason may well have been that the print was unsuitable for reproduction or that there were many pictures of the same type of article from which a choice had to be made.

Introduction

Many readers will be familiar with Mr Glenister's *Contemporary Design in Woodwork,* and it is hoped that this present book will meet a similar need in the field of metalwork.

In recent years there has been a growing public interest in the application of modern ideas of design to everyday things; many manufacturers have responded to this and each year has seen a wider variety of well-designed goods in the shops, competing with, and sometimes displacing, the ugly and shoddy. The photographs in these pages show some of the best present-day designs for articles in which metal is used. The criteria that the compilers have attempted to apply are that the objects included should be of recent manufacture, functional and of pleasing appearance; and that they should be soundly and economically constructed in the right material. In nearly every case the keynote is simplicity— a quality that demands, while it may conceal, great skill on the part of the designer.

Examples have been selected from a wide range of manufactures and from several overseas countries as well as Britain. Good design tends to be international but even so certain national characteristics are noticeable. The Scandinavian countries, for example, whose industries are largely craft based, handle stainless steel extremely well. Their cutlery and hollow-ware are rightly renowned. Similarly, the British tradition of fine craftsmanship in silver gives rise to some excellent new work from the hands of a new British 'school' of young designers.

The illustrations show how numerous problems of design have been resolved. It will be of interest to compare how two different designers have each produced his own answer in the design of any one article. In studying the pictures, allowance should be made for the fact that a photograph emphasises the visual appeal of an article but gives only a partial indication of its functional utility: and the latter quality is fundamental to good design.

The field of design in metalwork is wide, and constantly widening as a result of new technical developments. Malleable stainless steels, hard-surfaced aluminium alloys, plastic-coated metals—these and many other innovations have opened up fresh vistas for the craftsmen, designers, manufacturers and buyers of metalwork.

DINING CHAIR ▶

This interesting chair has legs of die-cast aluminium alloy of T section; the upholstered seat and back have sheet steel bases.

Designer Ernest Race, RDI, FSIA
Makers E. Race Ltd
Material Aluminium alloy
Finish Stove enamel

◀ TYPIST'S CHAIR

Seat height adjusts from 17 in. to 21 in.

Designer R. D. Rayfield
Makers A. Pegram Ltd
Material Mild steel tube
Finish Satin nickel plate

CHAIR ▶

Seat and back are tension springs covered with plastic tubing.

Designer Ernest Race, RDI, FSIA
Makers E. Race Ltd
Material Mild steel rod
Finish Stove enamel

◄ EASY CHAIR

A form which uses the resilience of metal; this Swiss chair has wide leather straps to provide a base for seat and back cushions.

Designer Robert Haussmann
Makers Haussmann and Haussmann
Material Steel strip
Finish Satin chrome plate

EASY CHAIR ►

The component parts of this chair from Denmark are joined with 'Unbrako' socket screws. As in the Swiss example the resilience of strip steel has been exploited.

Designer Poul Kjæholm
Makers E. Kold Christensen A/S
Material Mild steel strip
Finish Satin chrome plate

◄ EASY CHAIR

An American design made under licence, this unusual chair is of formed sheet steel with foam rubber upholstery. The exterior is white enamel.

Designer George Nelson
Makers Hille of London Ltd
Material Mild steel sheet and rod
Finish Enamel and chrome plate

EASY CHAIR ►

Designed for Gatwick Airport, this chair has foam rubber, leather-covered cushions on rubber webbing springing. The flush sides enable settees to be made up from individual units.

Designer Robin Day, RDI, ARCA, FSIA
Makers Hille of London Ltd
Material Mild steel square tube
Finish Satin chrome plate

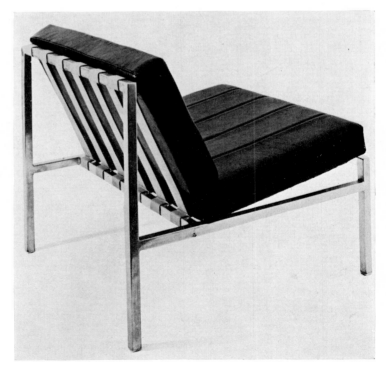

◄ EASY CHAIR

The main frame members are steel tubes; the seat cushion is supported on rubber webbing. Overall height 29 in., depth $26\frac{1}{2}$ in. and width 21 in. The arm rests are of mahogany.

Designer Jack Stafford, BSC (ENG) DIC
Makers Stafford Furniture Ltd
Material Mild steel tube and rod
Finish Matt stove enamel

ARM CHAIR ►

A pleasing combination of square sectioned steel tube and mahogany. Measures 22 in. wide, 26 in. deep, and 30 in. high.

Designer & Maker R. Henbest at Trent Park Training College
Material Steel tubing
Finish Matt enamel

◄ ROCKING CHAIR

This modern interpretation of a traditional chair is made entirely of welded rods.

Designer Ernest Race, RDI, FSIA
Makers E. Race Ltd
Material Mild steel rod
Finish Stove enamel

CANE CHAIR ►

This interesting chair is basically made from two steel rings.

Designer Frank Watkins
Makers Finmar Ltd
Material Mild steel rod
Finish Stove enamel

◄ OCCASIONAL CHAIR

The top of the back is of square steel; the seat is of formed ply, upholstered with foam interior.

Designer Jack Stafford BSC (ENG), DIC
Makers Stafford Furniture Ltd
Material Mild steel rod
Finish Stove enamel

◄ DINNER WAGON

Framework of square-section steel tubing. The trays are faced with melamine and edged with mahogany.

Designer Robin Day, RDI, ARCA, FSIA
Makers Hille of London Ltd
Material Mild steel square tube
Finish Bright chrome plate

DINNER WAGON ►

This trolley, 16 in. × 25 in. × 27 in. high, has a polished brass gallery and laminated plastic panels.

Designer John Bray LSIA
Makers Ferricane Furniture
Material Mild steel rod
Finish Stove enamel

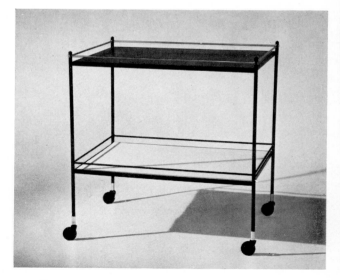

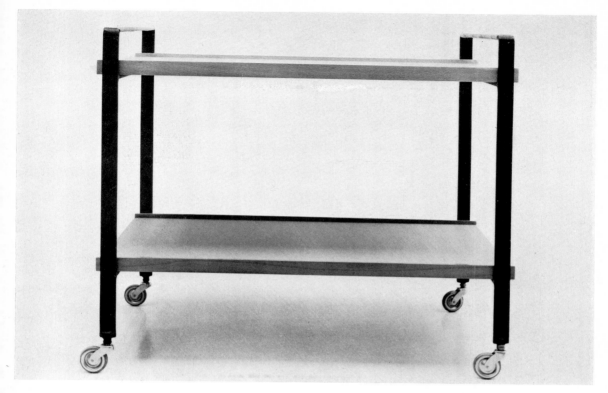

▲ DINNER WAGON

This simple design from Austria has a black strip steel frame, beech and laminated plastic trays and cane handgrips.

Designer & Maker C. Auböck
Material Mild steel strip
Finish Matt stove enamel

◄ DINNER WAGON

The removable trays are made of sheet steel with a bonded plastic surface. The handles are of beech.

Designer Martyn Rowlands
Makers Hygenic Wire Works Ltd
Material Steel rod and 'Stelvetite'
Finish Plastic

▲ STOOLS

Curved ply or upholstered seats are available. Heights 2 ft. and 18 in.

Designers Conran Design Group
Makers Conran & Co. Ltd
Material Mild Steel Rod
Finish Stove enamel

▲ HIGH STOOL

A welded construction of 7/16 in. rod, 26 in. high. The carved seat is of Agba.

Designers M. Collins and J. M. Spence
Makers Magpie Furniture Ltd
Material Mild steel rod
Finish Stove enamel

◀ STACKING TABLES

These tables, which also double as stools, have tops of hardwood or laminated plastic. Height 18 in.

Designer Gordon McClush
Makers Knoll International Ltd (USA)
Material Steel
Finish Stove enamel

CIRCULAR TABLE ►

The 3 in. diameter top is of ply with a laminated plastic veneer.

Designers Conran Design Group
Makers Conran & Co. Ltd
Material Mild steel tube, strip
Finish Silver bronze plate

◄ CIRCULAR TABLE

Brass-tipped legs and decorated 'Formica' top give added interest to this simple design.

Designer & Maker John I. Brooke
Material Mild steel rod
Finish Stove enamel

◄ CIRCULAR TABLE

The pedestal of this table (diameter 2 ft. 4 in., height 2 ft. 3 in.) is designed to take a sunshade. The top is of resin-bonded plywood.

Designer Ernest Race RDI, FSIA
Makers E. Race Ltd
Material Mild steel rod
Finish Stove enamel

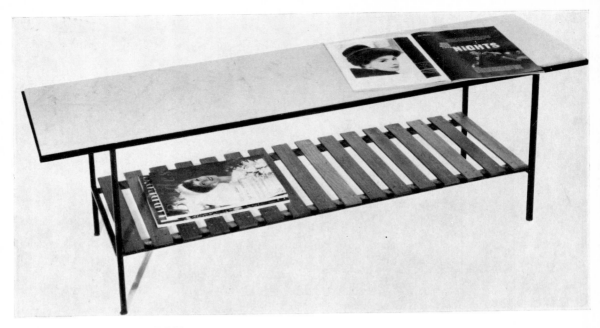

▲ OCCASIONAL TABLE

This marble-topped table, 4 ft. 8 in. × 14 in. × 18 in. high, has a magazine shelf of polished mahogany slats.

Designer & Maker Peter Cuddon
Material Mild steel square
Finish Matt stove enamel

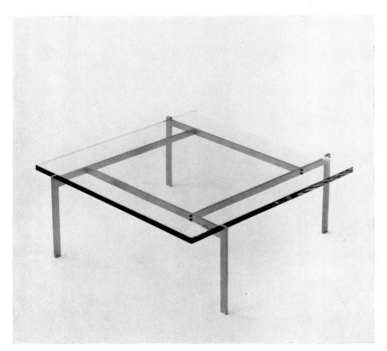

◄ GLASS-TOPPED TABLE

The underframing of this Danish table is constructed from four identical units joined with 'Unbrako' screws.

Designer Poul Kjæholm
Makers E. Kold Christensen
Material Mild steel strip
Finish Satin chrome plate

◄ TILE TABLE

Tables like this offer many decorative possibilities. The tiles, on a ply base, are held within an angle framework.

Designer & Maker Hamish Miller
Material Mild steel angle and rod
Finish Stove enamel

OCCASIONAL TABLE ►

The top of this table is made from sheet steel with a bonded surface of plastic, the ends are of beech.

Designer Martyn Rowlands
Makers Hygenic Wire Works Ltd
Material Steel rod and 'Stelvetite'
Finish Polythene covered

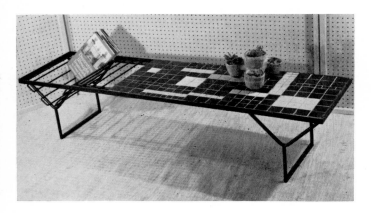

◄ TABLE

The legs and book rack are two interesting features.

Designer & Maker E. Heasman, at Goldsmiths' College, London University
Material Mild steel rod and angle
Finish Stove enamel

◄ WORK TABLE

Designed for use in school, this adjustable work table from Holland can be used sitting or standing. The various components are of channel section to give strength with lightness. Notice the additional surface for resting equipment.

Designer W. Rietveld
Makers de Cirkel N. V.
Material Mild steel
Finish Enamel

BOOKCASE ►

The shelves are made of plastic bonded steel folded to give a one-inch return, which makes them strong and neat in appearance.

Designer Martyn Rowlands
Makers Hygenic Wire Works Ltd
Material Steel rod and 'Stelvitite'
Finish Polythene covered

◄ KITCHEN TABLE

The use of three rods in each leg make stretchers unnecessary. The table top is of laminated plastic.

Designers & Makers Kandya Ltd
Material Mild steel rod
Finish Stove enamel

BUNK BEDS ►

Austere, typically Swiss, these simple bunk beds can be used separately. This is achieved with a square peg within the tube frame at the joint.

Designer & Maker Wohnhilfe, Zürich
Material Mild steel square tube
Finish Stove enamel

TWO EXAMPLES OF METAL USED
IN FURNITURE CONSTRUCTION

◀ DESK

In this desk aluminium angle section is
used to form the legs and top support

Designers & Makers L. M. Furniture
Ltd
Material Aluminium alloy
Finish Anodised

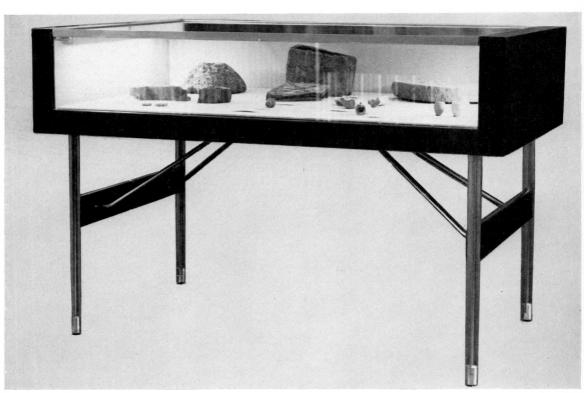

▲ DISPLAY CASE

Designed especially for use in God's House Tower Museum, Southampton, these display cases have
legs of X section aluminium alloy. Notice the feet.

Designers & Makers L. M. Furniture Ltd
Material Aluminium alloy
Finish Anodised

Furnishing Accessories

It is in this field that design is often at its weakest, the garish and shoddy most apparent. The clock that pretends to be a plate and the poker that hides behind a knight in armour, are only two examples of many. The following selection of photographs shows that the small things in the home—the clock, the ash-tray, the fire irons and so on—can be both well designed and attractive.

The examples here are taken from a wide range of products and in each case the designer has selected metals whose properties lend themselves best to the design. The items shown vary from specially commissioned work to mass-produced articles. Finishes are important if cleaning is to be kept at a minimum; thus, steel is stove enamelled, aluminium anodised and brass lacquered.

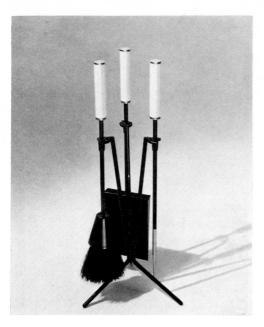

◄ FIRE IRONS

Tripod stand in mild steel of welded construction. Handles are white porcelain with brass fittings.

Designer Peter Cuddon
Makers Peter Cuddon Ltd
Material Steel
Finish Stove enamel

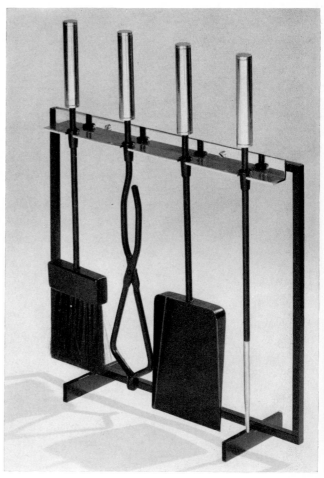

FIRE IRONS ►

The various tools are suspended from a brass rail by means of black P.V.C. grommets. The handles are of polished and lacquered copper tube.

Designer Peter Cuddon
Makers Peter Cuddon Ltd
Material Steel
Finish Stove enamel

PLANT STAND ▶

The polished mahogany trough has a removable steel lining and is suspended within the frame by polished and lacquered brass stays.

Designer Peter Cuddon
Makers Peter Cuddon Ltd
Material Steel
Finish Stove enamel

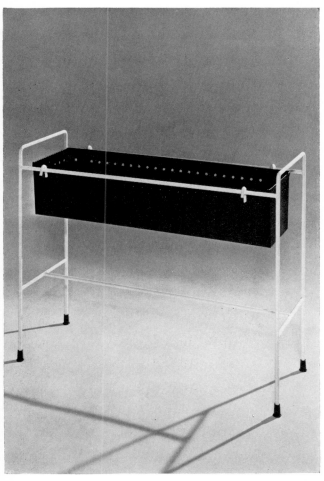

◀ PLANT STAND

Black trough and white stand 24 in. long, 8 in. wide and 20 in. high. P.V.C. feet. Notice how the end frames provide carrying handles.

Designer Peter Cuddon
Makers Peter Cuddon Ltd
Material Steel
Finish Stove enamel

◀ DISH

Hand-made in an interesting boat shape.

Designer Geoffrey Bellamy, DES RCA
Makers Bellamy & Tarratt
Material Silver
Finish Polished

◀ BOWL

From Norway. Diameter 15 in. Matt finish contrasts with polished cast silver centre decoration. Base of black marble.

Designer & Maker David Andersen
Material Silver
Finish Matt

▲ DISH

German. Made of heavy gauge sterling silver.

Designer Karl Dittert, DID
Makers P. Bruckmann & Söhne
Material Silver
Finish Polished

DISH ▶

Made of welded steel rods, with decorative cane binding; finished matt black.

Designer & Maker Laurids Lønborg
Material Steel rod
Finish Stove enamel

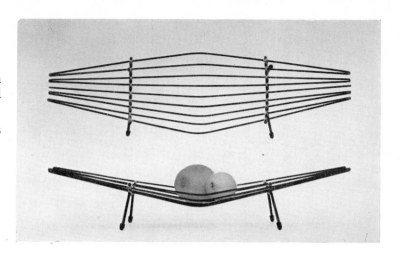

▲ VARIOUS DISHES

A collection of hand-beaten dishes, showing a wide range of possible shapes and sizes.

Designer & Maker John Grenville
Materials Stainless steel, copper and bronze
Finish Polished

◄ WALL CLOCK

Spun aluminium case. Diameter 9 in.

Designer Jack Howe, RDI, FSIA, FRIBA
Makers Gent & Co. Ltd
Material Aluminium
Finish Anodised

WALL CLOCK ►

Cast and turned brass bezel. Black engraved dial and brass hands.

Designers & Makers Baume & Co. Ltd
Material Brass
Finish Matt lacquer

◄ WALL CLOCK

Dark blue finished face, $8\frac{1}{2}$ in. diameter. From Germany.

Designers & Makers Gebrüder Junghans A/G
Material Brass
Finish Silvered

◄ CLOCK

The inside of the bezel is white, the face dark blue and the raised strokes and hands silvered. Diameter 7 in.

Designers & Makers Gebrüder Junghans A/G
Material Brass
Finish Polished and silvered

CLOCK ►

Diameter 6 in.

Designers & Makers Gebrüder Junghans A/G
Material Brass
Finish Matt nickel plate

◄ DESK CLOCK

Case partly covered with pigskin. Measures 5 in. × 4 in. × 2 in.

Designers & Makers Gebrüder Junghans A/G
Material Brass
Finish Polished and matt

◄ CIGARETTE BOWL

Bowl decorated with champleve enamel.

Designer & Maker A. H. Guise at the
   Royal College of Art
Material Silver
Finish Polished

CIGARETTE BOX ►

The engraved lines emphasise the interesting shape of this cigarette box. Actual size. Dutch.

Designer Gustav Beran, GKF
Makers Royal Van Kempen &
   Begeer
Material Silver
Finish Polished

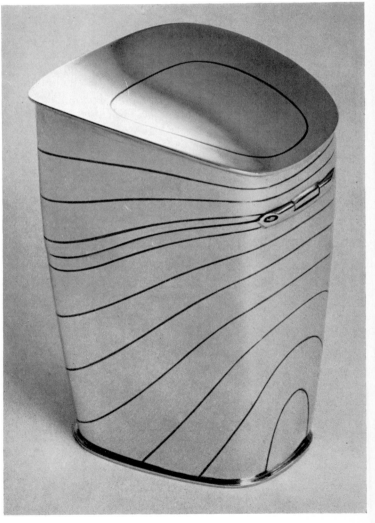

CIGARETTE BOWL ▶

Two identical units, one with punched decoration, the other plain. Danish.

Designers T. & E. Kindt Larsen
Maker A. Michelsen
Material Silver
Finish Polished

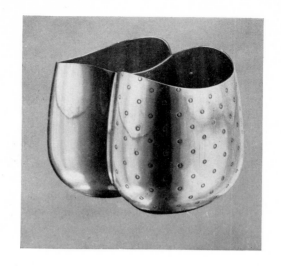

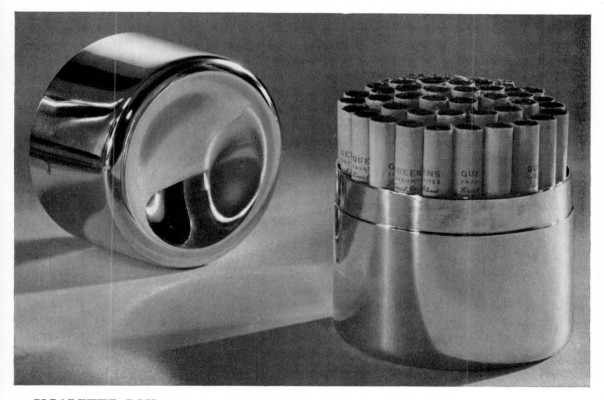

▲ CIGARETTE BOX

An example of fine silver from Denmark.

Designers Ibi Trier Morch
Maker A. Michelsen
Material Silver
Finish Polished

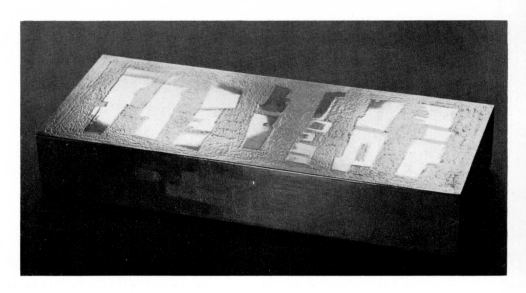

▲ CIGARETTE BOX

This simple box is given added interest by the use of an experimental etched surface decoration. (*Photograph*—Worshipful Company of Goldsmiths.)

Designer & Maker Desmond Clen-Murphy
Material Silver
Finish Etched and polished

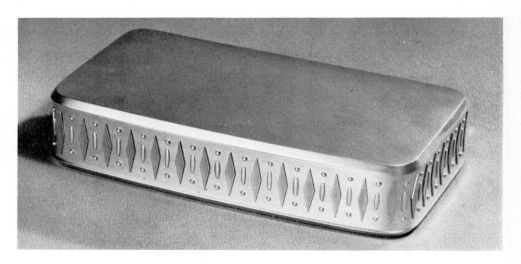

▲ CIGARETTE BOX

Parcel-gilt is silver decorated with gilding. Of particular interest is the lozenge shaped ornament. (*Photograph*—Worshipful Company of Goldsmiths.)

Designer & Maker David Mellor DES RCA
Material Parcel-gilt
Finish Polished

◄ BOX

A simple hinged box with slightly tapered sides enhanced by a freely engraved decoration.

Designer & Maker Eric Clements DES RCA, MSIA
Material Silver
Finish Polished

▲ WATCH CASES

Designed for Rolex of Geneva, these presentation watch cases with engraved motif are intended for re-use as pencil boxes.

Designer Milner Gray, RDI, FSIA
Makers D. & J. Wellby Ltd
Material Silver
Finish Polished

CANDLEHOLDERS

Candles are often used in Scandinavia for decorative lighting. These simple holders from Denmark are finished matt black and partly cane bound.

Designer & Maker Laurids Lønborg
Material Steel rod
Finish Stove enamel

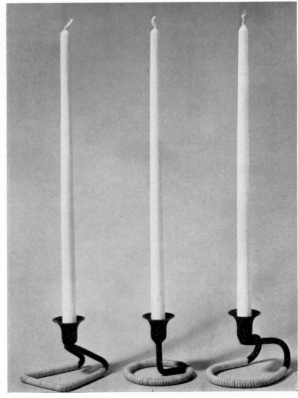

CANDLEHOLDERS

A group of designs showing brass used with wood—beech and teak. The holders on the right are cast and then turned, polished and lacquered.

Designer Kenneth Clark
Maker A. C. Brooker
Material Brass
Finish Polished

▲ ASH TRAY

Specially commissioned as a christening gift for godparents, this ash tray, of interesting shape, is 6¾ in. long. (*Photograph*—Worshipful Company of Goldsmiths.)

Designer & Maker Eric Clements, DES RCA, MSIA
Material Silver
Finish Polished

▲ ASH TRAY

This simple ash tray, a prototype for factory production, has an interesting black and bright anodised finish.

Designer & Maker Gerald Benney at the Royal College of Art
Material Aluminium
Finish Anodised

▲ ASH TRAY

The engraved inscription of this presentation ash tray is an integral part of the design. (*Photograph*—Worshipful Company of Goldsmiths.)

Designer Colin Toon
Maker Harry Brown
Material Silver
Finish Polished

◄ LOG BASKET

Welded steel rod. Woven cane handle.

Designer Desmond Sawyer, LSIA
Makers Desmond Sawyer Designs Ltd
Material Steel Rod
Finish Stove enamel

MIRROR ►

A table vanity mirror with a polished brass bezel, a bevelled mirror, and backed with felt. 16 in. tall and $7\frac{1}{2}$ in. wide.

Designer Colin Beales, ARIBA
Makers Peter Cuddon Ltd
Material Steel
Finish Stove enamel

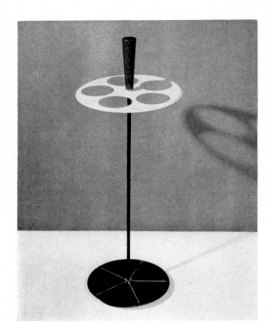

◄ UMBRELLA STAND

Sapele handle, coloured top, black stem and drip tray, and brass spreader.

Designer & Maker Hamish Miller
Material Steel and brass
Finish Stove enamel

UMBRELLA STAND ►

The sheet steel drip tray has wooden ends and is suspended on lacquered brass rods. Finish-matt black. 18 in. × 9 in. × 24 in. high.

Designer Peter Cuddon
Makers Peter Cuddon Ltd
Material Steel
Finish Stove enamel

Lighting

The design of domestic light fittings and lamps present two main problems. The first is functional efficiency, the second the full exploitation of the decorative possibilities offered in this kind of article. Function must always be the primary consideration.

Lighting can be roughly divided into two groups—diffused and directional. Amongst the first group are ceiling lamps, pendants and wall lamps. In the second group are lamps which provide a pool of strong light where and when required, for example, standard, desk, table and bedside lamps. Metal is widely used in the manufacture of all types of fittings: for shades of conical or cylindrical shape (usually of spun aluminium), stems of polished brass or stove enamelled steel tubing, and heavy stable bases of cast iron or lead. Hard-woods are often used in attractive combinations with these metals.

Concealed wiring, which greatly improves the appearance of any lamp, is contrived in many different ways. Ball, universal and knuckle joints enable many lights to be very flexible in use. The glitter of polished brass or anodised aluminium is appropriate and contrasts well with coloured, plain or textured shades.

◄ TABLE LAMP

Tapered stem and base insert of oiled teak.
Height 13½ in. without shade.

Designer Paul Boissevain DIP. ARCH, MSIA
Makers Merchant Adventurers Ltd
Material Aluminium
Finish Anodised

TABLE LAMP ►

Tapered stem of mahogany.

Designers & Makers Hiscock, Appleby & Co.
 Ltd
Material Brass tube
Finish Stove lacquer

◄ TABLE LAMP

Of unusual form, with an interesting shape of
shade, this lamp has two bulbs.

Designers & Makers Hiscock, Appleby & Co.
 Ltd
Material Brass tube
Finish Stove lacquer

◄ TABLE LAMP

The tripod base makes this lamp very stable, an important feature of design.

Designers & Makers Hiscock, Appleby & Co. Ltd
Material Brass
Finish Stove lacquer

DESK LAMP ►

Shade of spun aluminium

Designers & Makers Hiscock, Appleby & Co. Ltd
Material Aluminium and brass
Finish Stove lacquer

◄ TABLE LAMP

Black steel rods surround a brass centre stem. Overall height $23\frac{1}{2}$ in.

Designers & Makers Hiscock, Appleby & Co. Ltd
Material Brass and steel
Finish Lacquer and enamel

◄ DESK LAMP

The cast iron bases of these Danish desk lamps are both functional and decorative. The shade, which incorporates the bulb holder, can be adjusted to various positions. Height 14 in.

Designer Prof. Arne Jacobsen
Makers Louis Poulson & Co. A/S
Material Aluminium and cast iron
Finish Stove enamel

TABLE LAMP ►

The mahogany base of this simple table lamp is undercut to accommodate a steel weight. 'Raffitex' shade. Overall height 22 in.

Designers & Makers Hiscock, Appleby & Co. Ltd
Material Brass tube
Finish Stove lacquer

◀ DESK LAMP

The anodised aluminium wire base is covered with black plastic tubing. The shade, which is a standard component of this manufacturer's range, is 9 in. long and $5\frac{1}{2}$ in. in diameter.

Designers Yarborough & Holmes M/MSIA
Makers Cone Fittings Ltd
Material Aluminium
Finish Stove enamel

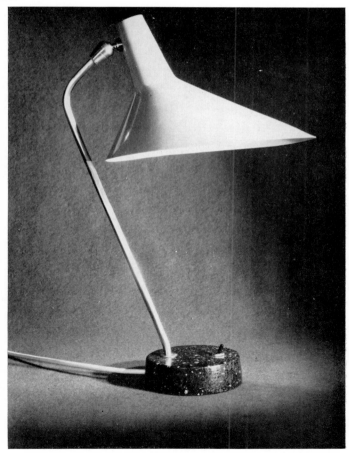

DESK LAMP ▶

This lamp with its interesting spun shade has a cast terrazzo base. The satin brass stem is lacquered to prevent tarnishing.

Designers & Makers Troughton & Young Ltd
Material Aluminium and brass
Finish Stove enamel

◄ WALL LAMPS

The shades can be turned once through 360° but no more; this prevents damage to the flex. The wall plaque is of hardwood.

Designers Yarborough & Holmes, M/MS
Makers Cone Fittings Ltd
Material Aluminium
Finish Stove enamel

WALL LAMP ►

Two swinging arms with a barrel joint and also a knuckle joint give this light a wide range of positions.

Designer Paul Boissevain, DIP. ARCH, MSIA
Makers Merchant Adventurers Ltd
Material Brass and aluminium
Finish Stove enamel and chrome

◄ WALL LAMP

Polished copper sleeves conceal the lamp holders.

Designers & Makers Troughton & Young Ltd.
Material Steel and copper
Finish Stove enamel

TWIN WALL LAMPS ►

This neat wall lamp has a hardwood cup and shades of pleated acetate. It is 20 in. wide and 12 in. high overall.

Designer Paul Boissevain, DIP. ARCH, MSIA
Makers Merchant Adventurers Ltd
Material Aluminium tubing
Finish Anodised gold

◄ WALL LAMP

Metalwork anodised gold.

Designer Noel Villeneuve
Makers Allom Heffer & Co. Ltd
Material Aluminium
Finish Anodised

WALL LAMP ►

The backplate, arm and ball joint are satin brass. The shade is 12 in. long.

Designer G. A. Scott
Makers The Maclamp Co.
Material Aluminium and brass
Finish Stove enamel

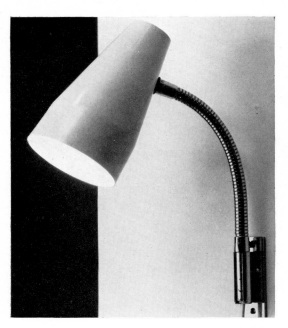

◄ ADJUSTABLE WALL LAMP

Flexible brass tubing has been carefully used here. Movement is also allowed at the wall bracket. Finnish.

Designer Lisa Johansson-Pape
Makers O/Y Stockmann
Material Aluminium and brass
Finish Stove enamel

►
ADJUSTABLE WALL LAMP

This ingenious wall lamp is adjustable to any position in a hemisphere, using a suspended balance weight. The arm is 36 in. long.

Designers Yarborough & Holmes,
  M/MSIA
Makers Cone Fittings Ltd
Material Aluminium and brass
Finish Stove enamel

◄ WALL LAMP

A simple construction of anodised aluminium sheet, this wall bracket measures 6 in. × 5 in.

Designers & Makers Troughton & Young Ltd
Material Aluminium
Finish Anodised

PORCH LANTERN ►

The diffuser is of white 'Perspex'. Overall height 9 in.

Designers & Makers G.E.C. Ltd
Material Sheet steel
Finish Stove enamel

◄ WALL LAMP

The diffusing fins are of acryl sheet. Finnish.

Designer Lisa Johansson-Pape
Makers O/Y Stockmann
Material Aluminium
Finish Stove enamel

◄ PENDANT LAMP

The handle is for adjusting height of lamp with counter weight (not shown).

Designers & Makers Troughton & Young Ltd
Material Aluminium
Finish Stove enamel

CEILING LAMPS ►

These lamps use contrasting painted and polished components for decorative effect. Finnish.

Designer Lisa Johansson-Pape
Makers O/Y Stockmann
Material Aluminium
Finish Polished

◄ PENDANT LAMP

The spun aluminium shade has an acryl diffuser. Finnish.

Designer Lisa Johansson-Pape
Makers O/Y Stockmann
Material Aluminium
Finish Stove enamel

◄ PENDANT LAMP

Composed of five standard components. The centre hub is of beech. The shades can be inverted.

Designers Yarborough & Holmes, M/MSIA
Makers Cone Fittings Ltd
Material Aluminium
Finish Stove enamel

PENDANT LAMPS ►

Matt enamel finish contrasting with a perforated brass trim make these 'chimney' type fittings decorative in addition to being functional. Finnish

Designer Alvar Aalto
Maker Artek
Material Aluminium
Finish Enamel

These standard lamps are examples of two different kinds of lighting—directional and diffused. Both have cast iron bases for stability.

Designers & Makers Hiscock, Appleby & Co. Ltd
Material Steel tube
Finish Stove enamel

SPOTLIGHT ►

Notice the carefully detailed brass ball and socket joint of this spun aluminium spotlight.

Designer John Hildred, MSIA
Makers G.E.C. Ltd
Material Aluminium
Finish Stove enamel

Tableware

The most interesting recent development in this section is the extensive use now being made of stainless steel. Still considered a new metal, high quality 18/8 (18% chrome, 8% nickel) steel is used for making a wide range of articles of tableware. In addition to its special property, stainless steel is robust in use, simply worked and easily cleaned, and it can have either a polished or a matt finish. The most successful pieces of design in stainless steel are those which do not attempt to copy forms used for other metals but stem from original and fresh thought.

In cutlery the short bladed knife is becoming more and more common; a logical development since only a short part of the knife is used when eating. Cutlery handles are frequently of new materials, such as nylon, and specially treated woods are also often used.

Well-designed tea and coffee pots combine attractive shapes and good proportions with functional efficiency: for instance, spouts that pour well without dripping, and handles that are comfortable without causing burnt fingers.

Silver, E.P.N.S. and pewter are used for hollow ware articles as well as stainless steel. Finishes are almost always highly polished but sometimes matt. Stove enamelled steel is used for such things as trivets and spirit-heaters.

◄ CUTLERY

Polished prongs, blade, and bowl contrast with matt finish handles. Notice the strengthening flute in the knife and spoon handles. Danish.

Designer Tias Eckhoff
Makers Georg Jensen Silversmiths Ltd
Material Silver
Finish Polished

CUTLERY ►

This German cutlery has nylon handles. The knife blade is worthy of note since a table knife is used to push, as well as cut, food.

Designer Karl Dittert
Makers Gowe-Metallwaren, GMbH
Material Stainless steel
Finish Polished

CUTLERY ▶

Austrian. The unusual tapered, matt-finished, handles contrast with highly polished parts.

Designer C. Auböck
Makers Ambosswerk Neuzeug
Material Stainless steel
Finish Polished

◀ CUTLERY

From Sweden. Notice the neat way in which the black nylon handles join the blades, giving a smooth finish which facilitates cleaning.

Designer Folke Arström
Makers Gense A/B
Material Stainless steel
Finish Matt polished

▲ FLATWARE

Polished and matt surfaces are used again in this cutlery commissioned by the S.A.S. airline. The handles are oval in cross-section.

Designer Sigurd Persson, SID
Makers Ko-operative Förbundet
Material Stainless steel
Finish Polished

FISH EATERS ▶

German flatware. The symmetrically bladed fish knife is unusual.

Designer Prof. Wilhelm Wagenfeld
Makers Württembergische, M/F
Material Stainless steel
Finish Matt polished

◄ CUTLERY

The tip of the knife blade is slightly serrated to give a better cutting edge. The handles are of palisander. Danish.

Designers Sigvard Bernadotte & Acton Bjørn
Makers Dansk Knivfabrik
Material Stainless steel
Finish Polished

CHILD'S SET ►

The centre bend in the handles helps both to stiffen and strengthen them. German.

Designer Günter Kupetz, DID
Makers Württembergische, M/F
Material Stainless steel
Finish Polished

▲ CUTLERY

Slim, square-sectioned handles of palisander wood. Notice the introduction of a distinct stem between handle and bowl.

Designer Tias Eckhoff
Makers Dansk Knivfabrik
Material Stainless steel
Finish Polished

◄ CUTLERY

Cutlery for special purposes. Hors d'œuvres fork, jam spoon and sardine fork with black nylon handles. Finnish.

Designer Bertel Gardberg
Makers Hackman & Co.
Material Stainless steel
Finish Satin polished

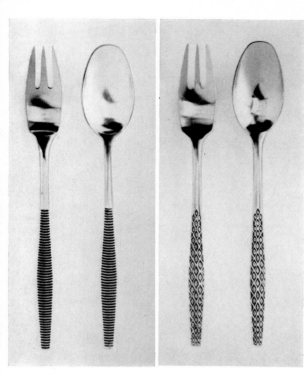

◄ FORK & SPOON

Identical forks and spoons, but with an interesting incised handle decoration filled black. Danish.

Designer Jens H. Quistgaard
Makers Dansk Designs
Material Stainless steel
Finish Polished

▼ CUTLERY

Square-sectioned handles of palisander wood. The small knife has an interestingly shaped blade. Finnish.

Designer Bertel Gardberg
Makers OY Fisuars A.B.
Material Stainless steel
Finish Satin polished

◄ SERVING SPOON

Notice the double pouring rim of this Danish spoon seen in two elevations.

Designer Tias Eckhoff
Makers Georg Jensen Silversmiths Ltd
Material Silver
Finish Polished

▲ SOUP LADLE AND SPOONS

A simple functional ladle for lifting and pouring liquids. The spoons are of solid silver.

Designer & Maker David Mellor at the Royal College of Art, London
Material Silver plate
Finish Polished

▲ SALAD SERVERS

From Germany. The form of the forked handle and the unusual shape of the bowl are interesting features. 8 in. long.

Designer & Maker Student at Kunstschule
    Krefeld (*Tutor* Hein Wimmer)
Material Silver
Finish Satin polished

▲ SALAD SERVERS

Interesting introduction of incised surface decoration on otherwise plain design. Danish.

Designer Jens H. Quistgaard
Makers Dansk Designs
Material Stainless steel
Finish Polished

▲ SALAD SERVERS

Bowl and fork forged from bar and then hollowed. Danish.

Designer Prof. Arne Jacobsen
Maker A. Michelsen
Material Silver
Finish Polished

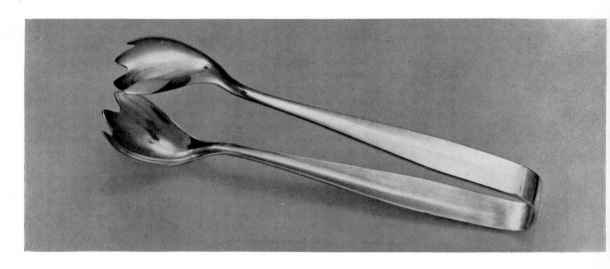

▲ SALAD SERVERS

Servers in the form of tongs. 8 in. long from Germany.

Designer Günter Kupetz, DID
Makers Württembergische, M/F
Material Brass
Finish Silver plated

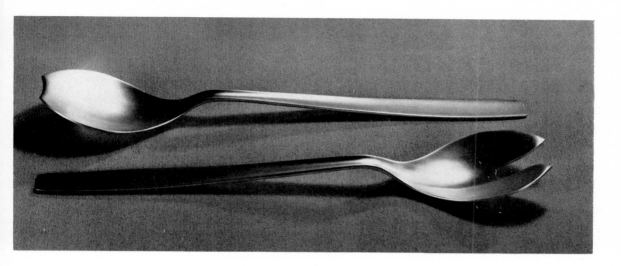

▲ SALAD SERVERS

The interesting feature of these servers is the way in which the handle has been fluted for part of its length to increase its strength. (*Photograph*—Worshipful Company of Goldsmiths.)

Designer & Maker J. B. Scott Smith
Material Silver
Finish Polished

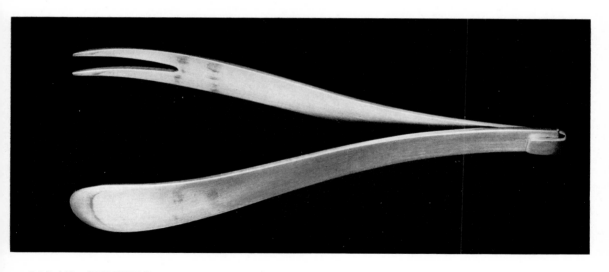

▲ SALAD SERVERS

The two parts of these tongs take apart for cleaning. Austrian.

Designer C. Auböck
Makers Ambosswerk Neuzeug
Material Stainless steel
Finish Matt polished

◄ TEA STRAINER

Machine-made with a moulded handle of black nylon. From Holland.

Designer Gustav Beran
Makers Royal Van Kempen & Begeer
Material Nickel Silver
Finish Electro plated

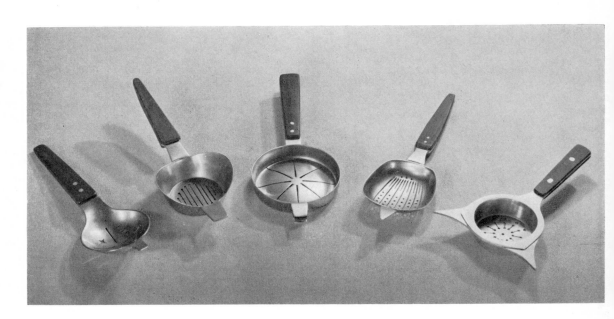

▲ TEA STRAINERS

Five design solutions to an everyday item of tableware. The handles are of rosewood. (*Photograph*—Worshipful Company of Goldsmiths.)

Designers & Makers Students at the L.C.C. Central School of Arts & Crafts
Material Stainless steel
Finish Polished

◄ KETTLE

This kettle has no lid and is filled through the spout. The handle is of moulded black plastic.

Designer & Maker Geoffrey Bellamy
   at the Royal College of Art, London
Material Gilding metal
Finish Polished

TEAPOT ►

The leather-covered handle is hinged, a feature common to several Scandinavian teapots and kettles. Danish.

Designer Erling Baruge
Maker Frantz Hingelberg
Material Silver
Finish Polished

◄ TEAPOT

Smooth flowing lines and fine craftsmanship. A teapot in the Scandinavian modern style.

Designer Henning Koppel
Makers Georg Jensen Silversmiths Ltd
Material Silver
Finish Polished

▲ TEAPOT

A prototype for quantity production in E.P.N.S., this teapot has a leather-covered handle and nylon knob. Notice the subtle shaping of the body and its relationship with spout and handle. (*Photograph* —Worshipful Company of Goldsmiths.)

Designer David Mellor, DES RCA
Makers Walker & Hall Ltd
Material Silver
Finish Polished

◄ HOT WATER JUG

The interesting cross-section, handle and ingenious lid are all details worth noting in this Danish design.

Designer Sigvard Bernadotte
Makers Georg Jensen Silversmiths Ltd
Material Silver
Finish Polished

TEAPOT ►

Fine craftsmanship and careful detailing are evident in this 2½-pint teapot. The handle is of purple-heart. (*Photograph*—Worshipful Company of Goldsmiths.)

Designer & Maker A. Hawkesley, DES RCA
Material Silver
Finish Polished

◄ TEAPOT

The lid of this German teapot incorporates a built-in strainer. The heating chamber contains a spirit heater.

Designer Karl Dittert
Maker Gebrüder Kuhn
Material Silver
Finish Polished

TEAPOT SET ►

A carefully detailed example of a teapot set, the like of which is often used in Europe, combining teapot, hot water jug and spirit heater.

Designer & Maker Hein Wimmer
Material Silver
Finish Polished

◄ COFFEE POT

Two interesting student designs. The handles and knobs are of black fibre. The height of coffee pots usually varies between $7\frac{1}{2}$ in. and $9\frac{1}{2}$ in.

Designer & Maker Stuart Renshaw at the
    Regional College of Art, Manchester
Material Silver
Finish Polished

COFFEE POT ►

Designer & Maker Cynthia Barlow at the
    Regional College of Art, Manchester
Material Silver
Finish Polished

◄ COFFEE POT

The handle and finial of this well-proportioned pot are covered in black morocco leather.

Designer & Maker Eric Clements, DES RCA, MSIA
Material Silver
Finish Polished

COFFEE SET ►

A heat-resistant, coloured nylon grip takes the place of the handles on these coffee and milk pots. The inside of the pot continues through the grip. (*Photograph*—Worshipful Company of Goldsmiths.)

Designer & Maker Stuart Devlin at the Royal College of Art, London
Material Silver
Finish Polished

◄ COFFEE SET

Simple shapes for easy factory production. Side handles and knobs of hardwood.

Designer Robert Welch, DES RCA
Makers J. & J. Wiggin Ltd
Material Stainless steel
Finish Polished

COFFEE SET ►

Once more simple shapes that are appropriate in stainless steel. The coffee pot has a cane bound handle. Danish.

Designer Lone Sachs
Makers Andersen & Burchardt
  A/S
Material Stainless steel
Finish Polished

◄ COFFEE POT

Cane covered handle. An interesting method of opening for one-handed use. Height 8¼ in. (*Photograph*—Worshipful Company of Goldsmiths.)

Designer & Maker Geoffrey Bellamy, DES RCA
Material Silver
Finish Polished

▲ COFFEE POT & MILK JUG

Handles of ivory and ebonised wood. A distinguished piece of design presented to the King and Queen of Denmark by the Queen and the Duke of Edinburgh, to mark their State Visit to Denmark in 1957.

Designer Eric Clements, DES RCA, MSIA
Engraver T. C. F. Wise
Makers Wakely & Wheeler Ltd
Material Silver   *Finish* Polished

◄ TEA CADDY

This fine caddy derives its elegance from subtle shape and surface finish. Notice how the careful detailing of the lid makes a knob unnecessary. Height $4\frac{1}{2}$ in. (*Photograph —Worshipful Company of Goldsmiths.*)

Designer & Maker David Mellor, DES RCA
Material Silver
Finish Matt polished

TEA CADDY ►

This caddy has several interesting features. The lid overlaps the body of the job, dispensing with a bezel. The lever knob is useful and decorative.

Designer & Maker Gerald Whiles at the
    Royal College of Art, London
Material Silver
Finish Polished

◄ CONDIMENT SET

An excellent example of modern English domestic silver. The cellars are $3\frac{1}{2}$ in. high. (*Photograph*—Worshipful Company of Goldsmiths.)

Designer & Maker Gerald Benney
DES RCA
Material Silver, parcel-gilt
Finish Polished

▲ CONDIMENT SET

From Denmark; engraved pots of equal size identified by ebony and ivory bases.

Designer Vagn Hemmingsen
Maker Frantz Hingelberg
Material Silver
Finish Polished

▲ CONDIMENT SET

The mustard dish is the same shape as the lower half of the cellar.

Designer Kenneth Clark
Maker A. G. Brooker
Material Silver
Finish Polished

◄ SALT & PEPPER POTS

A pleasing combination of teak and steel from Finland.

Designer Bertel Gardberg
Makers Hackman & Co
Material Stainless steel
Finish Polished

CONDIMENT SET ►

The decoration is engraved.

Designer & Maker J. B. Scott-Smith at the Royal College of Art, London
Material Silver
Finish Polished

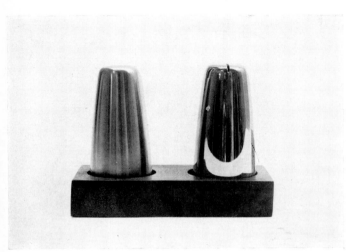

◄ SALT & PEPPER POTS

Identical pots except that one is polished, the other matt. Stand of walnut. From Austria.

Designer & Maker C. Auböck
Material Brass
Finish Nickel plated

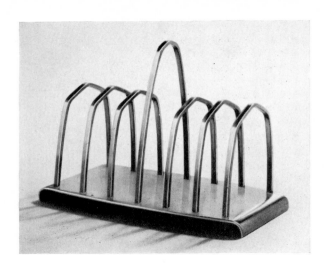

◄ TOAST RACK

A simple welded construction from square-sectioned and sheet steel.

Designer A. L. Wiggin
Makers J. & J. Wiggin Ltd
Material Stainless steel
Finish Satin polished

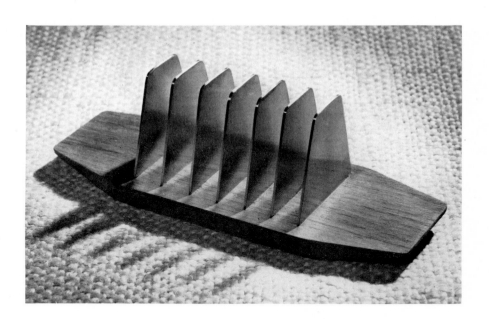

▲ TOAST RACK

Base of walnut. Tapered divisions fit into exact fit slots.

Designers & Makers Goodwood Metalcraft Ltd
Material Stainless steel
Finish Polished

TOAST RACK ▶

Ingenious construction and economical use of material are apparent in this mass-produced toast rack.

Designer Robert Welch, DES RCA
Makers J. & J. Wiggin, Ltd
Material Stainless steel
Finish Matt polished

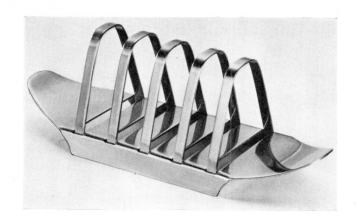

▲ TOAST RACK

Economical in use of material and in construction, this five-bar toast rack fully exploits the properties of stainless steel.

Designer John Brownsword
Makers Elkington Ltd
Material Stainless steel
Finish Matt polished

◄ SAUCE BOAT

An old material used in an interesting modern way. The decoration is knurled, and contrasts well with the polished surfaces and the hardwood handle.

Designer Gerald Benney DES RCA
Makers Viners Ltd
Material Pewter
Finish Part polished

▲ SAUCE BOAT

This small, carefully detailed, sauce boat is 7 in. long. The handle is worthy of note, especially the slight thickening. (*Photograph*—Worshipful Company of Goldsmiths.)

Designer & Maker Robert Welch, DES RCA
Material Silver
Finish Polished

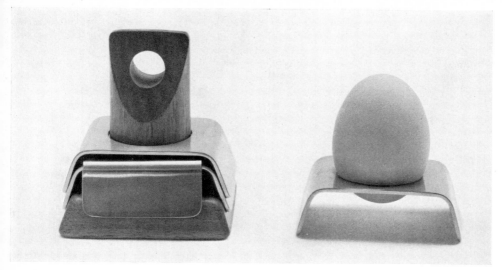

▲ EGG CUP

Complete simplification. Fresh thinking has led to this new conception of an egg cup. The equally simple rack is of hardwood. From Austria.

Designer & Maker C. Auböck
Material Stainless steel
Finish Matt polished

EGG CUP ▶

Mass produced, using two pressings, these stacking egg cups come from Germany.

Designer Prof. Wilhelm Wagenfeld
Makers Württembergische, M/F
Material Stainless steel
Finish Polished

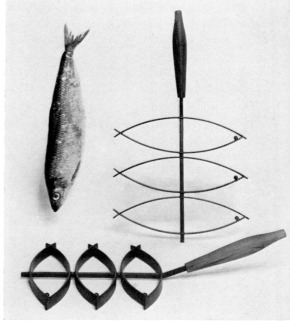

TRIVETS

Both functional and decorative, these Danish trivets have either cane bound or teak handles. Black matt finish.

Designer & Maker Laurids Lønborg
Material Mild steel
Finish Stove enamel

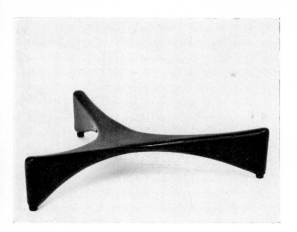

▲ TRIVET

Almost a sculptured shape, the flowing
lines and rounded corners necessary in
casting make this an elegant pot stand. It
has small rubber feet.

Designer Prof. Erik Herløw
Makers Ribe A/S Denmark
Material Cast iron
Finish Vitreous enamel

▲ SPIRIT WARMER

Of welded rod construction. Danish.

Designers & Makers Hejl & Co.
Material Stainless steel
Finish Polished

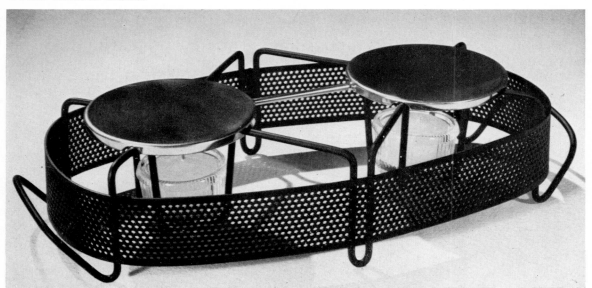

▲ PLATE WARMER

Of interesting construction from bent and welded steel rods. Brass cover plates diffuse the heat from
the candles. Swiss.

Designers & Makers Zug Metalwarenfabriken
Material Steel and brass
Finish Stove enamel

▲ WATER JUG

An interesting feature of this jug is the way in which the handle 'grows' out of the main body of the vessel.

Designer & Maker J. C. Shimeld at the Royal College of Art, London
Material Silver
Finish Polished

▲ DECANTER

A beautiful example of the silversmith's craft, this raised decanter is 8 in. tall and has an ivory stopper.

Designer & Maker John Grenville
Material Silver
Finish Polished

◄ MARTINI SET

Similar to the sauce boat from the same designer on a previous page. Note the bezel used to stiffen the rim.

Designer Gerald Benney, DES RCA
Makers Vimers Ltd
Material Pewter
Finish Part polished

WINE JUG & CUPS ►

Hand made, the jug has a 'neck' and no handle. Swedish.

Designer & Maker Sigurd Persson
Material Silver
Finish Polished

COFFEE URN & JUG

A one-gallon urn with a spirit heater. Handle, base and knob of rosewood. Presented to Churchill College, Cambridge, by Sir John Cockroft, the first Master.

Designer & Maker Robert Welch, DES RCA
Material Silver
Finish Polished

Ceremonial and Decorative Silver

Several articles made of silver appear in other sections of this book; gathered together here are items of ceremonial silver together with those of a more decorative kind. Much of the work has been specially commissioned and individually made by skilled designer craftsmen.

Silver trophies are commonplace, but those of good design are somewhat rare. A few examples of the latter are shown here, offering new ideas and shapes which are simple yet dignified. The photographs of candelabra and candlesticks show how many variations are possible with simple means.

The Church, so often in the past patron of the best contemporary artists and craftsmen, provides opportunities for silversmiths to design and make interesting modern articles for liturgical use. Jewellery is a field which obviously offers wide possibilities for decorative invention and experiment; and although only a few items have been included it will be noticed that simple, almost sculptural, shapes are much favoured.

Note. Since almost all of the items in this section are of silver with a polished finish these details have been omitted from the captions.

◄ SAILING TROPHY

A lively and very appropriate design. Here a decorative motif is completely integrated with the design and does not look as if it were added as an after-thought. (*Photograph*—Worshipful Company of Goldsmiths.)

Designer Alan Rawlinson
Makers Wakely & Wheeler Ltd

RUGBY TROPHY ►

Another sports trophy commissioned for a Scottish club. The bowl repeats the rugby ball shape. Rosewood base. (*Photograph*—Worshipful Company of Goldsmiths.)

Designer F. C. Bush
Makers Wakely & Wheeler Ltd

◄ TROPHY

A Rotary Challenge Cup from Holland. The cross-section is oval with a quarter twining twist and the knob of engraved crystal.

Designer Gustav Beran
Makers Royal Van Kempen & Begeer

TROPHY ►

Trophy, $10\frac{1}{2}$ in. tall, commissioned by the Worshipful Company of Gardeners for an annual competition. The refined decoration and the inscribed ring let into the wooden base are details worthy of note.

Designer Robert Welch, DES RCA
Maker T. Boucher

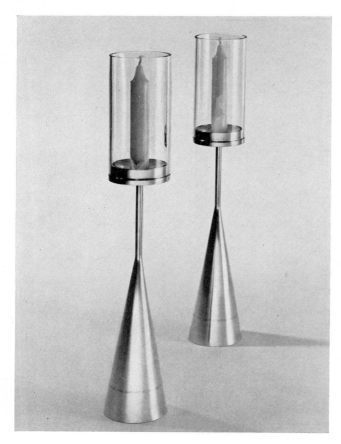

▲ CANDLESTICKS

Of silver plate, $15\frac{1}{2}$ in. high, this pair of candle-sticks were awarded to Mr. Neal French as the Duke of Edinburgh's Prize for Elegant Design, 1960.

Designer & Maker Robert Welch, DES RCA

TROPHY ▶

Amusing and yet refined is this trophy commissioned by the Duke of Edinburgh for a University Tiddlywink Championship. The wink, which is free to spin, has the Duke's coat of arms on the reverse. Height $15\frac{1}{2}$ in.; base of rosewood. (*Photograph*—Worshipful Company of Goldsmiths.)

Designer & Maker Robert Welch, DES RCA

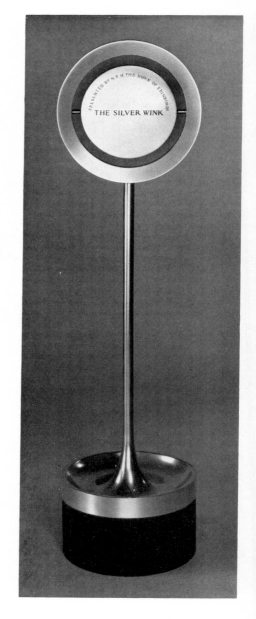

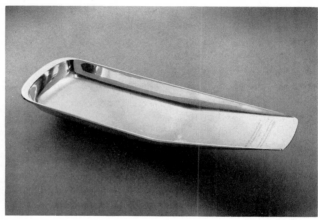

▲ FRUIT DISH

The Duke of Edinburgh's Prize for Elegant Design, 1959. It belongs to Mr. C. W. F. Longman, and measures 18 in. × 7 in.

Designer & Maker David Mellor, DES RCA

▲ TROPHY

A fine, stylish, and appropriate award. This trophy is presented annually by Ferodo Ltd for outstanding achievements in motor racing. Plinth of ebony and kingwood. (*Photograph*—Worshipful Company of Goldsmiths.)

Designer & Maker Gerald Benney, DES RCA

Material Gold 9ct.

◄ CANDLEHOLDERS

Three simple yet elegant candleholders in silver plate. Simplicity relies for success upon good proportions, as this example shows.

Designer Kenneth Clark
Maker A. C. Brooker

CANDLEHOLDERS ►

These candleholders from Germany have blue, green and red crystal drip dishes. Notice how the cross-section shape changes.

Designer Karl Dittert
Makers Württembergische, M/F

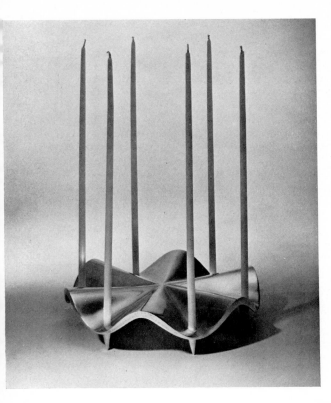

◄ CANDELABRA

An interesting and very decorative design. Overall diameter 12 in. From the Administrative Staff College, Henley. (*Photograph*—Worshipful Company of Goldsmiths.)

Designer & Maker Robert Welch, DES RCA

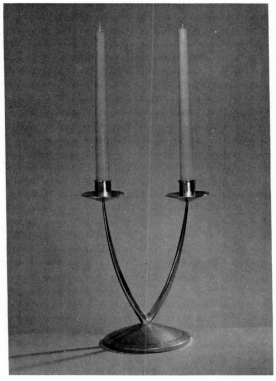

CANDLESTICK ►

Twin branched candlestick $9\frac{1}{4}$ in. tall. One of a set of three presented to the Administrative Staff College, Henley. (*Photograph*—Worshipful Company of Goldsmiths.)

Designer & Maker Gerald Benney, DES RCA

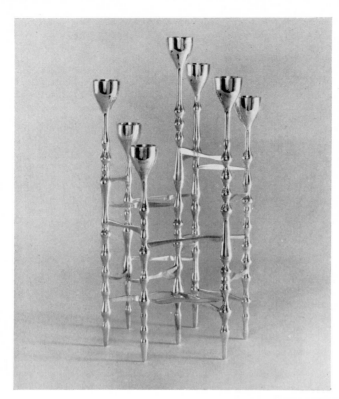

◄ CANDELABRA

A graceful, light and informal modern design. The differing height of the candle-holders gives added interest since the arrangement varies when viewed from different positions. Commissioned by the Worshipful Company of Goldsmiths. Height 18 in.

Designer & Maker Robert Welch, DES RCA

CANDELABRA ►

Almost an engineering approach to silversmithing is shown in this fine piece of work which belongs to the Sheffield Corporation. The base is of black marble.

Designer & Maker David Mellor, DES RCA

CANDELABRA ▶

A variety of levels gives added interest to this simple candelabra. Each holder has a ring of coloured enamel.

Designer Karl Dittert
Makers Württembergische, M/F

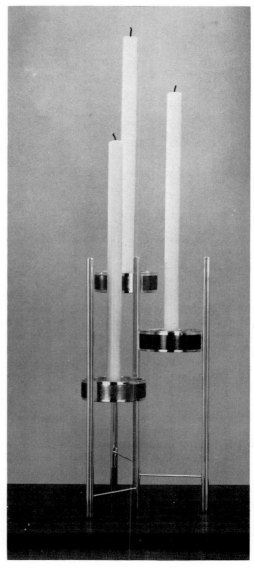

◀ CANDLEHOLDER OR VASE

Dual-purpose articles are rarely completely successful in both roles, but this 10 in. vase, because of its simplicity, works equally well as a candleholder.

Designer Arne Erkers
Makers Just Andersen A/S

◄ ALTAR CROSS

Contrasting matt and polished surfaces. The decoration is a large rock crystal in an ornamental gilt mount. From the Adolf Fredrick Church, Stockholm.

Designer & Maker Sigurd Persson, SID

▼ ALTAR CROSS & CANDLESTICKS

Cast silver cross and candlesticks with a deep etched textured decoration which contrasts with the highly polished outsides. From Gonville & Caius College Chapel, Cambridge.

Designer & Maker Gerald Benney, DES RCA

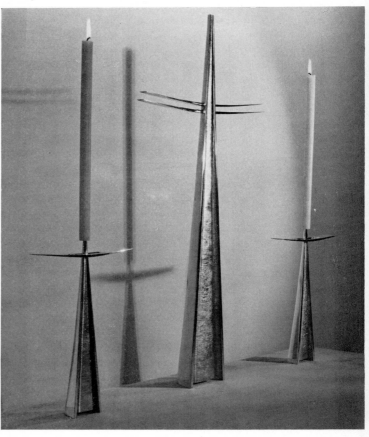

CIBORIUM ▶

Of sterling silver, fire gilt inside. Height 10½ in. From Coventry Cathedral. The steeple-like ferrule is pierced by two 'nails', a symbolic reference to the war-destroyed old Cathedral. (*Photograph*—Worshipful Company of Goldsmiths.)

Designer & Maker Gerald Benney, DES RCA

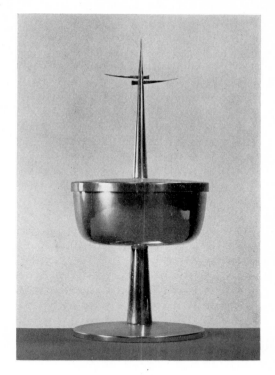

◀ CHALICE & CIBORIUM

Chalice and ciborium of identical design, one with a paten, the other with a lid. The knob on the stem has a traditional function. From St Mary's, Swansea.

Designer & Maker Robert Welch, DES RCA

CHALICE ▶

An unusual combination of metals, the cup is gold plated inside and the base is of cast iron with an as-cast finish. Height 7 in. From Germany.

Designer & Maker Hein Wimmer

◀ CHALICE

The hammer marks which have been left on the surface of the cup contrast with the gold plated inside and cast silver base of this chalice. Height 8 in. German.

Designer & Maker Hein Wimmer

◄ PATTEN

From Germany. The inscription is made up of fine silver wire. Diameter of bowl 7 in.

Designer & Maker Hein Wimmer

 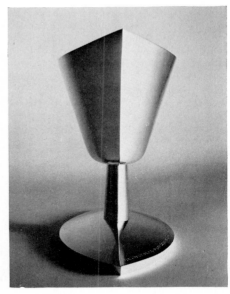

▲ ALTAR VASE

Two views of an altar vase for St Mary's, Swansea. In silver plate; the sharp edges give a crisp appearance.

Designer & Maker Robert Welch, DES RCA

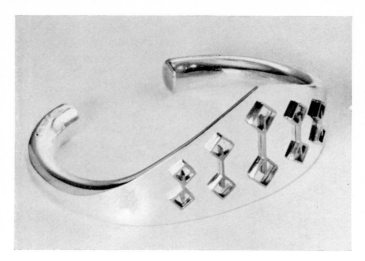

◄ BRACELET

From Finland. The applied decoration is of gold on silver.

Designer & Maker Bjorn Weckstrom

BRACELET & NECKLACE

▶

Danish, a modern design made up from interlocking identical components. The bracelet is probably more successful functionally than the necklace.

Designer Søren Georg Jensen
Makers Georg Jensen Silversmiths Ltd

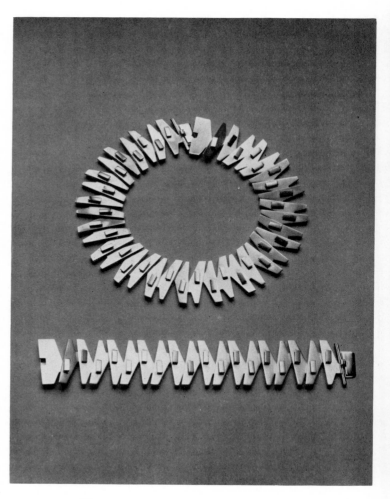

RINGS ▶

Three rings with semi-precious stones. Absence of usual claw mountings gives clean appearance. From Germany.

Designer & Maker Hans Markl
Material Gold

▼ BROOCH

Gold with pearls of different colours. Once again a simple but very effective design. Twice full size. Swedish.

Designer & Maker Sigurd Persson, SID

◄ PENDANT

A cast silver pendant with a pearl from Norway. Much interesting jewellery is made by casting, and very intricate designs are possible when centrifugal casting equipment is used.

Designer & Maker Gudmund J. Elvestad

◄ PENDANT

From Sweden. Small pieces of silver strip have been fused together and then mounted on a highly polished concave back plate. Actual size.

Designer & Maker Carl Nystromer

PENDANT ►

A sculptured asymmetrical shape, a moonstone and a black pearl are the components of this German pendant.

Designer & Maker Hans Markl

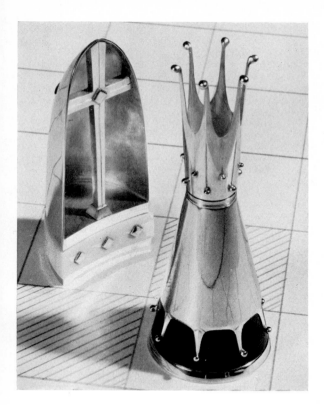

◄ CHESS PIECES

Queen and Bishop, an example of modern decorative metalwork. The sets distinguished by ivory or rosewood bases. Heights 3¾ in. and 3 in.

Designer & Maker Cynthia Barlow at the Regional College of Art, Manchester

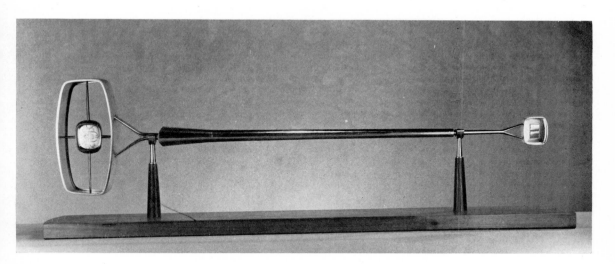

▲ MACE

Presented by the City of Leicester to Leicester University. Made in sterling silver, parcel gilt. Length 4 ft. 3 in. Stand of teak with silver clasps. (*Photograph*—Worshipful Company of Goldsmiths.)

Designer & Maker Gerald Benney, DES RCA

◄ VASE

Two identical sides seamed together; viewed here in side elevation.

Designer Tapio Wirkkala
Makers Kultakeskus. OY

▲ ROSE BOWL

Uncompromisingly modern, this rose bowl was commissioned by the Directors of the National Bank of Scotland and presented to Lord Rowallan, K.T. The inside of the bowl and the upright rings are of gilt. (*Photograph*—Worshipful Company of Goldsmiths.)

Designer & Maker Gerald Benney, DES RCA

Wrought Ironwork

On the following pages will be found a few examples of recent wrought ironwork made in a school and in colleges and by a master smith. By the nature of the material and the processes involved, the designs must inevitably have a traditional flavour, and the working of scrolls still forms the basis of decorative treatment. The work of the wrought iron smith is still largely carried out by hand methods.

Hence it is expensive to produce, demand tends to be small and designers generally lacking in initiative. Moreover, the market is flooded with cheap and shoddy factory-made imitations, some of which use bent wire and strip metal welded together. Probably in no other field of present-day metalwork is there so much undistinguished or even bad design, or so little that is really 'contemporary' in feeling.

◄ GATES

The simple rectangular shape has been sub-divided and parts filled with a repeated scroll decoration.

Designer & Maker S. J. Stringer at Goldsmiths' College

▲ GATES

The overall shape of these gates is of particular interest. The decoration is based on the repetition of a simple unit.

Designer & Maker E. W. Heasman at Goldsmiths' College

◄ GATES

Scroll work is once again used to add interest to these gates of simple form.

Designer & Maker Joseph Gurtner

SINGLE GATE ►

Designer & Maker Joseph Gurtner

▲ SIGN BRACKET

Simple scroll forms both support and decorate this bracket.

Designer & Maker J. Gilder at Trent Park College

◄ SINGLE GATE

Designer & Maker K. Collison at Trent Park College

ROOM SEPARATORS & BALUSTRADE

Light and elegant, these two examples avoid the heavy appearance that is sometimes associated with ironwork.

Designer & Maker Joseph Gurtner

▲ EXAMPLES OF SCROLL WORK

These units show how scrolls can be arranged to form decorative motifs.

Designer & Maker W. Alton

BOOT SCRAPER ▶

A sturdy and practical item.

Designer Ronald Duffield. Made at Bingley County Secondary School

◄ FIRESCREEN

Simple and restrained decorative scrolls have been used in this screen. The background is of fine gauze.

Designer Ronald Duffield. Made at Bingley County Secondary School

▼ SIGN

An outdoor symbol for the Cambridge Instrument Company. The centre part is polished.

Designers Edward D. Mills & Partners, Architects
Maker Raymond Lister

◄ CROSS

Extremely simple and yet very effective, especially against the background of fair-faced brickwork. Note the punched outlining.

Designers Hughes & Bicknell, Architects
Maker Raymond Lister

▼ GRILLE

From Coventry Cathedral in the form of a 'Crown of Thorns'.

Designer Sir Basil Spence
Makers The Royal Engineers

Miscellany

Metal is used in a hundred different ways, and many articles of good design do not easily fit into the well-defined groups of the previous sections. Gathered together here is a selection of photographs to show a few of the many ways in which designers have tackled the problem of making things of metal. They include tools, domestic equipment, architectural metalwork and street furniture.

Traditional tools are usually well designed, since time has proved both function and shape. The selected photographs here, however, show how some tools can be improved upon and refined by designers who take a fresh look at the design problems involved. Many tin and galvanised kitchen utensils are being replaced by those made of plastics, but at the same time, new plastic-sprayed or coated steels have opened up many interesting possibilities. Improved methods of anodising aluminium have led to the increased use of this important but often misused material, especially in the manufacture of door furniture.

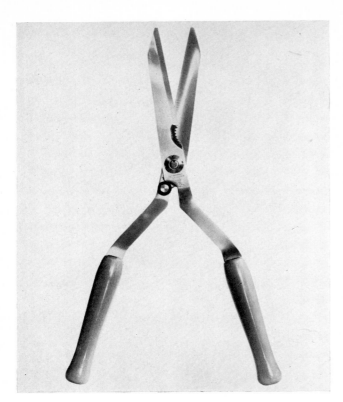

◄ SHEARS

These shears incorporate several interesting features. The cranked handles make cutting less laborious. They have a rubber cushion stop and floating bearings. The beech handles have hidden ferrules.

Designers & Makers Wilkinson Sword Ltd
Material Carbon steel
Finish Matt chrome plate

PRUNER ►

A much more tidy design for this type of article than ever before. The handles are of aluminium alloy stove enamelled.

Designers & Makers Wilkinson Sword Ltd
Material Carbon steel
Finish Matt chrome plate

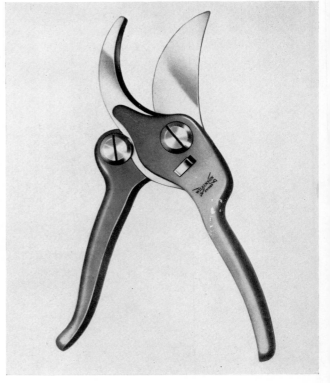

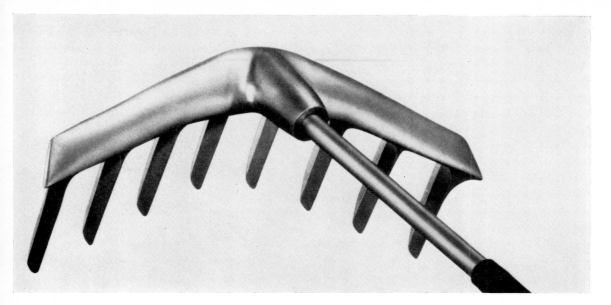

▲ RAKE

An improvement upon the conventional rake. The swept-back design draws the earth together, avoiding overspilling. The steel tang is welded into a tubular steel handle.

Designers & Makers Wilkinson Sword
  Ltd
Material Aluminium bronze
Finish Polished

HOE ▶

Of unusual design, this hoe—called a 'Swoe' by its makers—has three cutting edges.

Designers & Makers Wilkinson Sword
  Ltd
Material Carbon steel
Finish Chrome plate

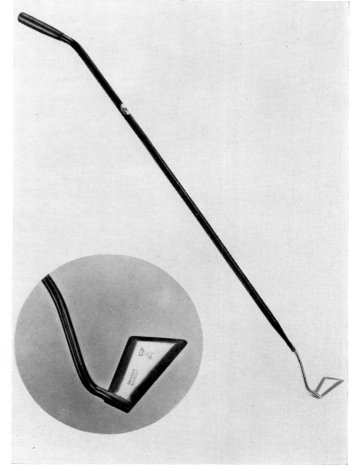

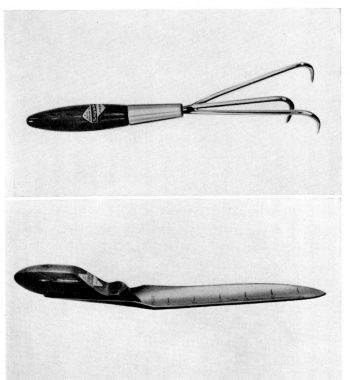

◄ CULTIVATOR AND TROWEL

Garden tools of stainless steel repay extra expense by long life. The trowel is graduated for planting purposes.

Designer H. J. Dowsett
Makers Stainless Developments Ltd
Material Stainless steel
Finish Polished

HAND FORK AND
   TROWEL ►

The blades of these tools are roll-forged. Notice that the blades and tang are one piece. Beech handles.

Designers Mellor & Asquith
Makers Spear & Jackson Ltd
Material Steel
Finish Satin chrome

CHISEL ▶

This carefully detailed design incorporates several new features. A steel shaft runs through the plastic handle joining the blade to the steel cap.

Designers & Makers Ward & Payne Ltd
Material Tool steel
Finish Polished

▲ REBATE PLANE

This hand-made plane has a hard-wood filling between the side plates.

Designer & Maker Kevin Plunkett at Goldsmiths' College, London University
Material Steel
Finish Polished

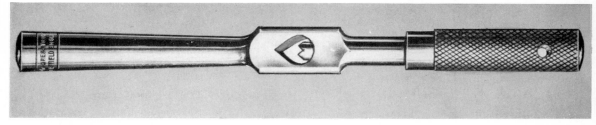

▲ TAP WRENCH

This tap wrench, unlike most others, grips the square shank of the tap on both sides by means of a spring-loaded centre rod.

Designers & Makers Moore & Wright Ltd
Material Steel
Finish Part polished

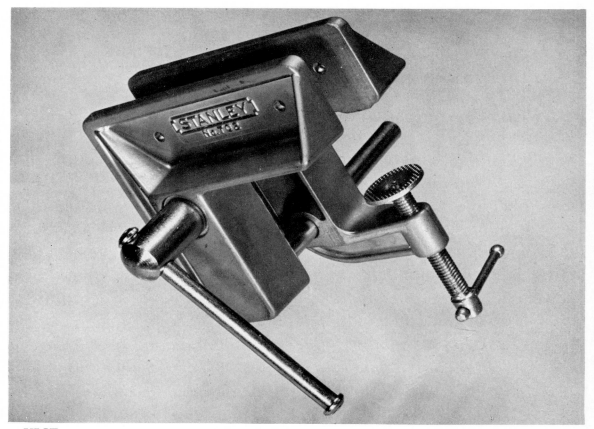

▲ VICE

This portable and very adaptable vice is of die cast aluminium alloy and chrome plated steel. Jaw capacity $3\frac{1}{2}$ in.

Designers & Makers Stanley Tools (G.B.) Ltd
Material Aluminium alloy
Finish Japanned

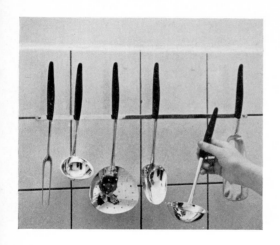

KITCHEN TOOLS

These Dutch cooking implements, of simple line and fine finish, have black nylon handles which incorporate a hanging hook; this hook also prevents them slipping into cooking pans.

Designer Gustav Beran
Makers Royal Van Kempen & Begeer
Material Stainless steel
Finish Polished

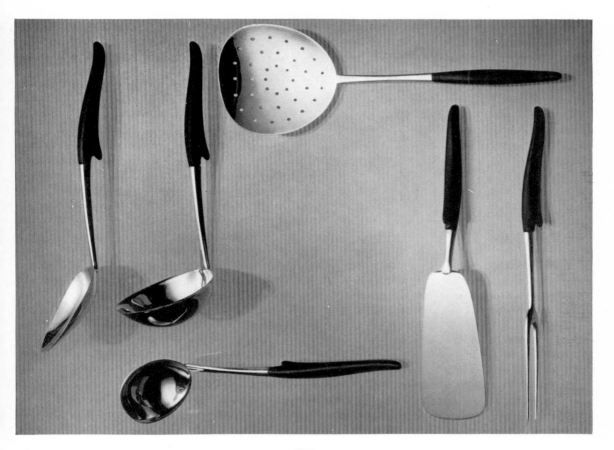

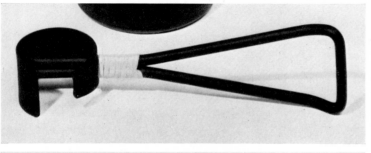

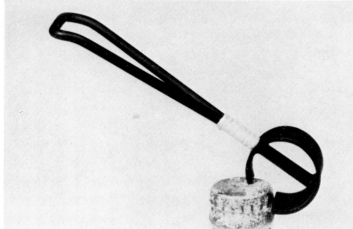

◀ BOTTLE OPENER

Two views of an interesting crown cap opener from Denmark.

Designer & Maker Laurids Lønborg
Material Mild steel
Finish Stove enamel

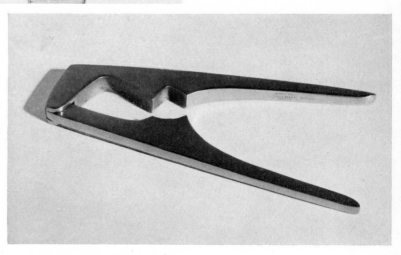

▲ NUTCRACKERS

Refinement and improvement upon a conventional design are evident here.

Designer Robert Welch, DES RCA, MSIA
Makers J. & J. Wiggin Ltd
Material Stainless steel
Finish Polished

◀ MILK CRATE

The hinged flaps, which prevent birds removing caps, come up to form a carrying handle.

Designers & Makers Hygenic Wire Works Ltd
Material Steel rod
Finish Plastic

WINE RACK ▶

A sturdy construction of welded steel rods.

Designer Desmond Sawyer, LSIA
Makers Desmond Sawyer Designs Ltd
Material Steel rod
Finish Stove enamel

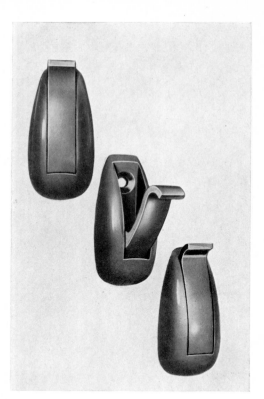

◄ COAT HOOKS

Designed for use in the B.O.A.C. Comet aircraft, these coat-hangers of die cast aluminium alloy are spring-loaded to snap closed when not in use.

Designer L. B. Suter
Makers The Birmingham Guild Ltd
Material Aluminium alloy
Finish Stove enamel

▼ TOWEL RAIL

The roller is of porcelain. Fixing by means of concealed nylon cleats screwed to the wall.

Designer Peter Cuddon
Makers Peter Cuddon Ltd
Material Aluminium alloy
Finish Anodised

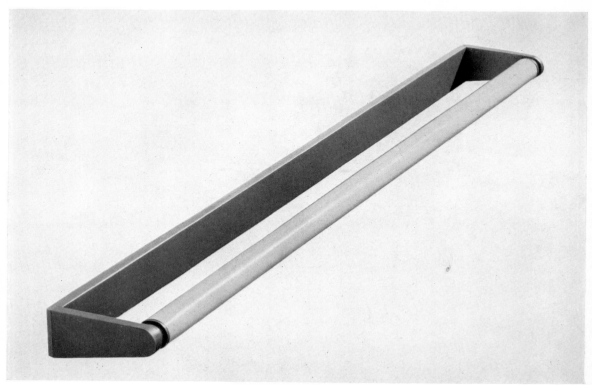

DOOR KNOCKER ▶

Of cast aluminium alloy. Door knockers of good modern design are rare.

Designers & Makers Dryad Metal Works Ltd
Material Aluminium alloy
Finish Anodised

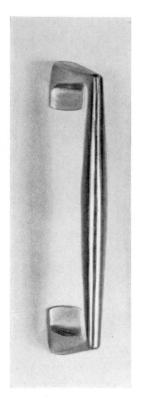

▲ DOOR PULL

Designers & Makers Dryad Metal Works Ltd
Material Aluminium alloy
Finish Anodised

DOOR PULL ▶

Incorporates polished hardwood grip

Designers & Makers James Gibbons Ltd
Material Aluminium alloy
Finish Anodised

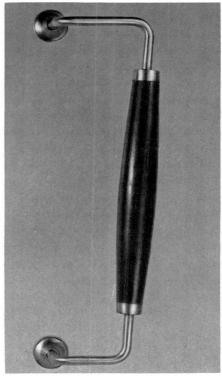

DOOR LEVERS

Designers & Makers James Gibbons Ltd
Material Aluminium alloy
Finish Anodised

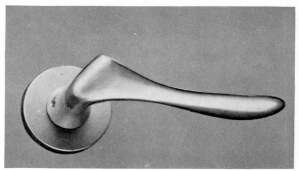

DOOR LEVER ▶

Well designed levers are comfortable to grip, pull, push and turn.

Designer Roger Peach, FSIA
Makers Dryad Metal Works
Material Aluminium alloy
Finish Anodised

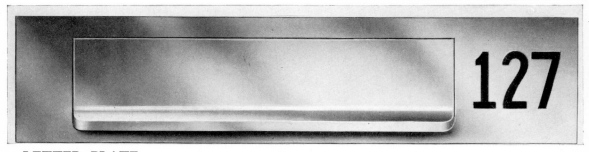

▲ LETTER PLATE

Die cast. The flap lifts outwards. The numbers are cast with the back plate.

Designer W. H. Hall, MA, PH D
Makers Sundaw Products Ltd
Material Aluminium alloy
Finish Anodised

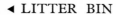

◄ LITTER BIN

The hinged lid is of fibreglass. Note the neat foot.

Designer David Mellor, DES RCA, for National Benzole Ltd
Material Sheet steel
Finish Stove enamel

LITTER BIN ►

A neat design solution; this bin is 2 ft. 6 in. high and of 10½ in. diameter.

Designer Derek Goad & John Ricks
Makers G. A. Harvey Ltd
Material Perforated sheet steel
Finish Galvanised and painted

◄ LITTER BIN

This bin with U-section legs is 2 ft. 6 in. high and 3 ft. 6 in. diameter.

Designer Derek Goad & John Ricks
Makers G. A. Harvey Ltd
Material Perforated sheet steel
Finish Galvanised and painted

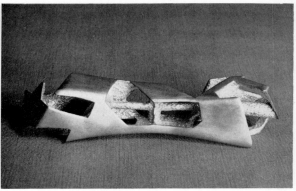

▲ DECORATIVE CASTINGS

These experimental castings are made by carving a core after an impression has been made in sand, then replacing the core and pouring.

Designed & made at Goldsmiths' College, University of London (*Tutor:* G. L. Morgan)
Material Zinc alloy (Kayem)

▲ SCREEN

Organ screen at Barking Methodist Church. The connecting pieces are of turned brass.

Designer George Baines & Syborn—Architects
Makers Wainwright & Waring Ltd
Material Aluminium
Finish Polished

Names and addresses of manufacturers and craftsmen

Allom Heffer & Co. Ltd, 17 Montpelier Street, London S W 7
Andersen & Burchardt, Grundtvigsvej 29, Copenhagen, Denmark
Andersen, David, Carl Johans Gt., Oslo, Norway
Andersen, Just, Gammel Kongere 3, Copenhagen, Denmark

Baume & Co. Ltd, 1 Hatton Garden, London E C 1
Bellamy & Tarratt, 19 Market Street, Leicester
Benney, Gerald, Suffolk House, Whitfield Place, London W 1
Birmingham Guild Ltd, Grosvenor Street West, Birmingham 6
Brooke, John, 5 Manfred Road, London S W 1 5
Brooker, A. G., 4 Church Vale, Forest Hill, London S E 2 3

de Cirkel, Zwanenburg, The Netherlands
Clark, Kenneth, 29a Clipstone Street, London W 1
Clements, Eric, 15 Beaks Hill Road, Kings Norton, Birmingham 30
Cone Fittings Ltd, 9 Rosemont Road, London N W 3
Conran & Co., 5 Hanaway Place, London W 1
Cuddon, Peter, 58 Princess Victoria Street, Bristol 8

Dansk Designs Ltd, 22 Grosvenor Street, London W 1 1
Dansk Knivfabriken, Grundtvigsvej 29, Copenhagen, Denmark
Dryad Metalworks Ltd, Sanvey Gate, Leicester

Elkington & Co. Ltd, 52 Grosvenor Gardens, London S W 1

Ferricane Furniture, Conyer Quay, Teynham, Kent
Finmar Ltd, 26 Kingly Street, London W 1

G.E.C., Magnet House, London W C 2
Gent & Co. Ltd, Faraday Works, Leicester
Gense A/B, Eskiltuna, Sweden
Gurtner, Joseph, Low Well Forge, 47 Briggate, Shipley, Yorks
Gibbons, Jas., Ltd, St Johns Works, Wolverhampton
Goodwood Metalcraft Ltd, Chichester, Sussex
Grenville, John, Clare, Nr. Sudbury, Suffolk

Hackman & Co., Glogatan 3, Helsinki, Finland
Harvey, G. A. & Co. Ltd, Woolwich Road, London S E 7
Hawksley, Anthony, Dragon House, Deddington, Oxford
Hille, 39/40 Albemarle Street, London W 1
Hingleberg, Frantz, Store Torv. 5, Aarhus, Denmark
Hiscock, Appleby & Co. Ltd, 12 Holbein Place, Sloane Square, London
    S W 1
Hygenic Wire Works Ltd, Miles Road, Mitcham, Surrey

Jensen, Georg, A/S Regnagade 7, Copenhagen, Denmark
Junghans, Gebrüder, Schramberg, Germany

Kandya Ltd, Hayes, Middlesex
Knoll International Ltd of USA, 2 Ridgmount Place, London W C 1
Kuhn, Gebrüder, Kalter Market 18, Schwäbisch, Gemünd, Germany

Lister, Raymond, 180 Chesterton Road, Cambridge
L. M. Furniture, Wallingford, Berkshire
Lønborg, Laurids, Fortunstraede 3, Copenhagen, Denmark

Maclamp Co., 56 Church Road, Acton, London W 3
Magpie Furniture Ltd, Station Approach, Mortlake, London S W 1 4
Markl, Hans, Ludenscheider Weg 4E, Berlin, Germany
Mellor, David, 1 Park Lane, Sheffield 10
Merchant Adventurers Ltd, Feltham, Middlesex
Michelsen, A., Sturlasgade 14, Copenhagen, Denmark
Miller, Hamish, Tanyard Lane, Steyning, Sussex
Moore & Wright, Handsworth Road, Sheffield 1 3

Pegram, A., Ltd, 183 Royal College Street, London N W 1
Persson, Sigurd, Hogbersgatan 12, Stockholm, Sweden
Poulsen, Louis & Co. A/S, Nyhavn, Copenhagen, Denmark

Race, Ernest, Ltd, 22 Union Road, Clapham, London S W 4
Ribe Jernstoberi, Ribe, Denmark

Sawyer, Desmond, Designs Ltd, Topsham, Devon
Spear & Jackson Ltd, Savile Street, Sheffield 4
Stafford Furniture, 19/21 Leicester Square, London W C 2
Stag Cabinet Co. Ltd, Hadyn Road, Nottingham
Stainless Developments Ltd, 65 East Barnet Road, New Barnet,
    Hertfordshire
Stanley Tools (G.B.) Ltd, Rutland Road, Sheffield 3
Stockman/Orno, Keskuskatu 2, Helsinki, Finland
Sundaw Products Ltd, 108 Union Street, Smethwick, Birmingham 4 0

Troughton & Young Ltd, 143 Knightsbridge, London SW1

Van Kempen & Begeer, Zeist, The Netherlands
Viners Ltd, Bath Street, Sheffield 1

Wainwright & Waring, 14 Mortlake High Street, London SW14
Walker & Hall Ltd, Electro Works, Sheffield 1
Ward & Payne Ltd, 5 Hillsborough, Sheffield 6
Welch, Robert, The Mill, Sheep Street, Chipping Campden, Gloucester-
    shire
Wiggin, J. & J., Bloxwich, Walsall, Staffordshire
Wilkinson Sword Co., Southfield Road, London W4
Wimmer, Hein, Alte Forststrasse 2 Rath-Heumar, Cologne, Germany
W.M.F., Geislingen, Steige, Germany